MW01289086

SCARS OF BLESSING

Christie Layne

Large Print

Eleos Press

First Printing: Scars of Blessing
Author: Christie Layne
© 2016
All rights reserved.

This book or parts thereof may not be reproduced in any form, stored in a retrieval system, or transmitted in any form by any means without prior written permission of the author, except as provided by United States of America copyright law.

Cover Art and Design: Eleos Press
Interior Formatting: Eleos Press

www.eleospress.com

ISBN-13: 978-1523292615

PRINTED IN THE UNITED STATES OF AMERICA

Jesus is the Way Maker

Love
Christie
Lamp

SCARS OF BLESSING

On March 1, 2010, I went to work like any other day. I managed a Tire shop. I have been there for nine and half years. It was approximately one thirty in the afternoon. I was told that I came out on the floor and asked the guys why they weren't working on that tire and rim that were sitting there. They told me they couldn't get it to bead up. So I picked up the tire with the rim. I walked over to the tire machine and placed the rim and tire on the table and clamped it. I hooked the airline to it. I grabbed both sides of the tire to hold it in place while stepping on the foot lever to add the air. I stepped on the lever; the bottom side of the bead on the tire exploded, causing the tire and rim to pull off the machine. The explosion was so powerful the table top on the machine broke off. I was told that the tire and rim left the machine came up to my face and body. The tire and rim then went through me continued on up to the ceiling and caved in a heater in the ceiling.

I was told the explosion was so loud it was like a huge bomb. I was thrown on the floor and a lady who worked inside the store came out as soon as she heard the explosion. She was the first one to me. She said I was lying there, my face covered in blood. My arm was broke completely into, and my hand was hanging down to my elbow holding on by the small piece of skin. She told me I was trying to get up off the floor when she got to me. She asked me what I was trying to do. And I told her I was trying to get up to see what had happened in the shop that something had happened and I had to get out there. She informed me that I had blown my arm off and I needed to lay still.   That's when I started panic and screaming.

Well, right as the explosion took place there was an off-duty husband and wife paramedical team that had come in to check prices of tires. They had walked up to the counter when they heard the explosion. The husband was the first paramedic to start toward me. He yelled at his wife and said call for ambulance. When he got to me and saw what all had happened. He told her, "This is bad. Call for an air lift chopper." I was told that there happened to be an ambulance sitting just across the highway that was there in seconds. When they were putting me in the ambulance, the lady who had worked inside said she could hear me screaming all the way in the store. I was also told about a year-and-a-half later that the helicopter was already in the area flying back to Nashville from another drop off.

They had me in Vanderbilt Hospital within minutes. When my husband Harvey got the call that I had been hurt he was 100 miles NW of Nashville. He turned around and headed back to Nashville. He pulled in when they were taking me into emergency surgery, trying to save my arm. Harvey was told that they reattached my arm with two metal plates and 13 screws. Sewed up the gash in my forehead, I had a broken rib on my right side, a bruised liver, my sinus was fractured; all the bones around my eyes and in my face had multiple fractures. My pupil in my left eye was much bigger than the right, and I was seeing three times the objects in that eye. My pinky finger on my right hand had been broke numerous times. They put a long pin in it to hold the bones together till they healed. I also had a hole, the size of a nickel, in the back of my head, where I had been thrown back onto the concrete floor. Harvey was told I might not make it through the night.

After surgery they put me in the trauma unit. Harvey was sitting with me. When he noticed that my arm was rising like a loaf of bread. He called for the nurse. I had gone into compartment syndrome. My arm was swelling fast. They took me back in surgery to open my arm, to relieve pressure. They had to or I would have lost my arm.

In the meantime my mom and dad were on their way with my fifteen-year-old son. Michael got to the hospital. Harvey brought him in to see me. It was not something a mother would want her son to see. I was told he stood by my bedside looking at his mom, who looked like something out of a horror movie. He grabbed the side of my bed and started shaking. He asked them "Why would God allow this to happen to my mama?" My mom told him, "God didn't allow it to happen. She is going to be ok. God will take care of her." With that, I was told he relaxed and looked at mom. He said, "Yeah, He will."

I was also told that the waiting room was full of the guys from work. Their families were there too. What an honor to have so many people in my life, to care so much for me!

Harvey said he woke me up about three a.m. on March the second to see if I would respond. I wasn't at myself. I laid in trauma for a few days. There were people who said they came and visit me and prayed with me. I remember no one. They said I had lots of visitors. I wish I could remember everyone that came by to see me. I do remember looking across the trauma room and seeing a man lying in bed with a metal halo attached to his head. I ask the nurse what happened to him. She told me that he had been in a bad motorcycle accident. He had been hit by a car on each side at the same time and he was paralyzed from the neck down. He would never walk again.

The next day I could hear crying on the other side of the curtain next to me. I ask the nurse why those people were crying. She said, "Well, the man in the bed on the other side of the curtain, had been hurt in a logging accident." "He was cutting a tree when it jumped and took half his face off." "His family is telling him bye because they are going to unplug his life support machine."

I laid in trauma for a few days. It was approximately five days they moved me down to the burn unit. That was the only place they had to put me. I'm still not quit at myself. But I was able to carry on a conversation. I was lying in bed and was starting to get restless, starting to really get sick of this whole thing. I was asking God why this happened to me. What had I done to deserve this? Why was I being punished? When, all of sudden, I heard this loud crying. The nurse came through the door. I hatefully asked her why was that baby crying out so loudly. She said, "Mrs. Layne, I'm so sorry if that is bothering you. It is an eleven-month-old baby—his step-father threw him into scolding hot water. He is in a lot of pain; we are trying to comfort him and calm him down." With that, I laid back on my bed. I looked up and asked the Lord to forgive me. Here I was—alive. My arm had been reattached, and I had a good chance of being able to use it. I could speak and tell others where I was hurting. I said, "Please forgive me, Lord."

The next day I was sitting in bed. I was really getting uneasy sitting there. Harvey was over in the chair next to my bed. I was moving and tossing and squirming. I was really getting fed up with the whole situation. I heard this sweet little voice say, "Hello!" I looked over at Harvey. I knew it wasn't his voice, so I turned toward the door— which was open a little; there, sitting in an orange and yellow plastic car, was a little boy, covered from head to toe with gauze. He had a smile that shined brighter than any sunshine I had ever seen. I said hello and he went on his way. The nurse came in. I ask her, "What is going on with that child?" She said that he had fallen in a camp fire and had been burned from head to toe. We let him ride around in that car because it keeps his mind off his pain."

When she told me that, I just started crying and asking God to just forgive me. Here were these little ones, going through what promised to be some very bad trauma. One of them couldn't speak to tell anyone what misery he was in. How sad to be such an innocent child, and to be mistreated that way. Yet another had such a big, bright smile on his face, even though he was covered from head to toe with very bad burns that were wrapped in gauze; he was riding around, smiling, from room to room, cheering up the other patients—like me—who were sitting there feeling sorry for themselves. God is an awesome God.

I started just praying for these children, and asking God to forgive me, for being so self-centered. Please Lord Watch over these children. Bless them and give them strength. Lord. Help me to be more like the little boy who is riding around in the toy car, spreading smiles and joy, instead of just feeling sorry for myself. Little ones surely can teach us grownups a lot in a short period of time.

I was told that I was a very blessed lady. I was told I had so many visitors. I really wish I could remember them all. I was told by the nurses that phone calls were coming in so much that they just couldn't deliver all the messages. I was told that prayers were going up across the United States and back. I was told that members of the Christian Motorcycle Association came by to see me, and made me an honorary member. They came by and prayed with me. They had heard they had a rider that had fallen.

My husband stayed with me through thick and thin. A friend of mine came and stayed a couple nights during my stay at the hospital. My very dear friend came while I was in trauma and helped Harvey clean me up. I am such a Blessed lady. I am so rich when I look back and count all the friends family and sisters and brothers in Christ I have.

They had now, by this time, moved me to the round room. This is where I spent the last three days of my thirteen-day stay at Vanderbilt.

I had one more surgery on my arm. They had to do a skin graph from my leg to put on my arm. After the graph took I was released to go home.

They wheeled me out of the front door of the hospital. I can honestly say I have never seen the world through my eyes the way I saw it that day. Everything was so bright. I could have had on four pairs of sun glasses and still would have to squint with my eyes. Everything had a whole new look. I told Harvey everything was so beautiful and bright. What an amazing God we have, to show me a whole new world. No matter where I looked, everything looked new and fresh. I have often won-dered if that is the way Noah and his family felt when they stepped out of the ark.

Well, April the first was my first appointment. I went to Vanderbilt. When I stepped off the elevator the first person I saw was the man who was in trauma same time I was that had been in a motorcycle accident. He was in a wheel chair. I remember I was told by the nurse he was paralyzed for life. Well, I walked up to him; I said, "Excuse me, but were you in the trauma unit on the first week of March?" He said, "I was." I said, "Well, I was told that you were in a bad motorcycle accident, and that you were paralyzed from the neck down." He looked at me and said,

"No, I'm not," and he picked his leg up and moved it as he shook his arms and hands. He said, "I got a long way to go, but I'm not going to be paralyzed. I will walk and I will have a normal life."

I was called back for my appointment they took x-rays of my arm. The doctor came in and told me that my arm was missing over a quarter of an inch of bones; that they would have to do surgery and take bone out of my leg and put it in my arm. I remembered the man I saw when I got off the elevator. I looked at the doctor and said I will not do the surgery. The doctor informed me that I had no choice that if my bones don't connect I will lose use of my arm. I looked at the doctor square in the face and something came over me, and I told him I declare it in the name of the Lord right now I will not have this other surgery. My bones will grow. The doctor looked at me and said, "I believe in the work of the Lord but, Mrs. Layne, you are missing over a quarter of an inch in both bones; it is not possible for them to grow in time to keep you from losing your arm." I looked at him with a stone face and said, "I declare it in the name of the Lord my bones will grow; I will not have this surgery." He said, "Ok, Mrs. Layne I will give you four weeks. If your bones do not show rapid growth, we will do the surgery." I said, "Doctor, I will take that and I will tell you now you will not do this surgery." With that, I walked out and went home.

On April the second, I started my occupational therapy. I had no idea what this would consist of. It took hard work, determination, and discipline. When I started there, I could not bend a finger, could not bend my wrist, and could not do anything with my right arm. I told the therapist that my goal was to be in the Trail of Tears the third week in September. I told her that when I accomplish that I have overcome this trauma physically.

"Satan has tried hard to get to me through this whole ordeal. I ride the Trail of Tears every year. I have for several years. It is so special to me. See, when I ride my motorcycle that is my time with my Lord and Savior. It is so special because it is just me and him. No phones, no one talking, no interruptions. It is just me and him. I try to put into words what it feels like to just be on the bike and talking to him, all the while riding through his creations he has given me to enjoy. That is such a bonding time with me and my Savior. We have talked through a lot of worries, happiness, and rejoicing on that bike. "

I was going to therapy three days a week. I could not drive due to my head injuries. So between my friend and my son who had just recently got his drivers permit? God is so good. They would get me to therapy. I would work hard for three hours. When I was done, the pain was unbearable. I would have to take pain pills just to ease it off. Then I would walk behind the building where I was taking therapy, because I couldn't drive. I would go to my friend's house, which had just moved there in February right before my accident. I would go in and rest, while the pain pills had eased my pain, when my friend got off work she would take me home.

It didn't dawn on me till sometime later that God had provided a place for me to go when I got out of therapy. I couldn't drive, and I would have to wait on her to get off work. God knew when he put her in that house that I would be taking therapy next door.

He knew I would need a place to rest and that I would have to wait till someone could get me home. God is so good.

On April fifteenth I went back to doctor in Nashville to see if the bone in my arm had grown any. When I got there, they took x-rays and I waited in the room on the doctor. He walked in with x-rays in his hand, and said, "Mrs. Layne, I can't explain what I am seeing, but your bone has really shown rapid growth; if it continues on at this pace, we will not have to do the surgery." I told him I could explain it easily. "It was the Lord. I declared in the Lord's name that my bone would grow—and it did—because I had faith." The doctor started laughing, and said, "Yes, you did."

Satan was still trying to get in the door. A bacterial infection had set up in my arm. They put me on stronger antibiotics, and it knocked it right out in no time. I continued with my therapy, and I really had to lean on the Lord through this.

Sometimes I would leave there thinking, "Wow, I'm really making progress." Other times, it was rough trying to come to grips that you got to learn how to use one of your limbs all over again, and to look at it and see the stitches and the wounds. The pain was unbearable most of the time. All through this, the Lord was using different people in my life to keep me encouraged. I would receive at least five cards a day through the mail from people I didn't have any idea even knew me. The phone calls kept coming every day. People would bring food. The Lord is so good to me. I would have never thought I was so rich when it came to brothers and sisters in Christ and friends and family in my time of need. God is so good.

Harvey and I were talking about my accident and my stay in the hospital; I was struggling hard trying to remember the details. We were talking about how the Savior had been there for me. How the ambulance just happened to be across the street, almost like it was waiting. How the paramedics just happened to walk in to check prices of tires.

I was talking to Harvey about the man who had been in the motorcycle accident—that the nurse had told me he was paralyzed from the neck down. I also told him about the logger the nurse said his family was telling him, "Bye," because they were going to unplug his machine, and the two little boys in the burn unit. I was talking to Harvey about how it was the same nurse in both rooms. He asked me what I was talking about. I said, "Well, every time she spoke to me she whispered in my ear." I said, "You know—she wore the bright white uniforms like the nurses used to wear back in the day. It was so bright that every time she bent down to speak to me it glowed brightly around my face." Harvey looked at me and said, "Christie, there was no such nurse in either of your rooms at any given time."

I knew then that God had sent me an angel to help me through my stay at the hospital. I believe in my heart that he had her to tell me about the guy in the halo to give me hope, and to give me a stronger faith. I believe he had her tell me about the logger on the other side of the curtain, to show me that could have been my family telling me, "Bye. To hang in there, 'cause he wasn't done with me yet." I believe he had her to speak to me about the little children to show me that I needed to stop complaining, stop feeling sorry for myself, and to praise him, no matter what the circumstances are. Yes I knew in my heart that God had sent me an angel. Man what an awesome feeling to realize that God speaks to you in so many ways and forms. If we would just take time and be still and listen to the whisper, and open our hearts to his love for us.

My next appointment was set for May thirteenth the doctor had told me at the last appointment that he wanted me to be able to make a fist when he saw me on this appointment. I was trying really hard in occupational therapy to work on it. It was a real challenge, that I was really having a hard time with. When my appointment day rolled around, the doctor's office called and said they would have to postpone my appointment due to flooding in Nashville.

I had also taken my last pain pill that morning. I didn't have any idea what was headed my way. As the evening approached I was starting to need another pain pill. See I was on the strongest pain pill that could be prescribed. The night time set in, so did the pain. But that wasn't all that was going on. I didn't realize that I had gotten addicted to the pain pills I was on. My skin started crawling; my body felt like it had strange things crawling through it. I couldn't set down. I was walking sometimes even trotting through the house. All I wanted to do was out run it. I would go outside and just fast walk around the house. I would come back in and just walk and walk and walk. No matter how hard I try, I could not out run it. I would even climb in the shower with my clothes on and just claw at my body trying to pull whatever that was crawling through my body out. Michael, my son was here and he would ask me what is wrong. "Mama, what is wrong? Why can't you sit down?" I told him I didn't know. I didn't know what was going on. I told him to go to bed. "Don't worry—I'm ok." Later on that night, it got so bad. I walked down the hall to where we keep a loaded pistol on top of a clock. I slowly reached up on the clock took down the pistol. With tears streaming down my face, I was telling Jesus I couldn't do this anymore. I can't take no more. As I went to raise the pistol to my head, I heard Michael's bedroom door open. I looked down the hall. Michael asked me," Mom, you ok?" I said, "Yes, son, I'm ok. You go back to sleep." He turned and went back to his room. I put the pistol back on the clock. Then I crawled back in the shower and just cried and clawed at my skin. Later on that night, I walked back down the hall. I reached up on top of the clock and got the pistol as I went to raise it to my head. I heard Michael's door open. I looked down the hall. Michael asked again, "Mom, are you ok? I said, "Yes, son, I'm ok. You go back to bed and rest. I'm ok."

The night went on. It was getting into the early morning hours. I just could not take any more. I walked down the hall got to the clock. Reached on top and got the pistol. As I went to place it against my head, I heard Michael's door open. I looked down the hall, and there stood Michael. He asked for the third time, "Mama, are you ok?" I said, "Yes, Michael, I am ok." He said, "Mom, I love you." I said, "I love you, too, baby. Go back to bed." With that, he turned and went into his room. I started crying so hard. I hit my knees, and begged God to forgive me. "Forgive me for only thinking of myself. Forgive me for not being stronger. Forgive me for even thinking of taking my own life, when you spared me through that terrible accident in March." God showed me that Michael would have been the one to find me. Michael never gets out of bed once he is asleep. I have known him to do it once in a while, but never three times in one night. God spoke to me through Michael.

I made it through the night. I called the doctor's office as soon as I could the next day. I spoke with the nurse, and told her I needed something to be called in for pain—but I did not want the pills they had me on. She said, "Mrs. Layne, you cannot stop taking those just like that—you will have a massive heart attack." They then started taking steps to step me down off of the pills they had me on.

I always thought that people who were addicted to pills or alcohol or anything. That it wasn't as bad to stop as they say. Well I was wrong. It is rough, and you truly need God to get through it. I have a whole new respect for people with addictions.

I continued with my therapy. My appointment was coming up on May twentieth. I was working hard trying to make that fist. It was not an easy task. I went to my appointment. They took x-rays; I waited in the room. The doctor walked in. He said, "Let me see that fist." I gritted my teeth; I closed my eyes, In hopes of being able to do it. I squeezed as hard as

I could. Every bend just over run with severe pain, the doctor said it is not a tight fist, but a good attempt at a fist. Then he looked at me with a smile on his face and said, "Mrs. Layne, I was looking at your x-rays. Your bones have touched." I yelled, "Praise God, praise God."

He said the devil was still trying to get in there. My arm had set up another infection. The doctor put me on stronger antibiotics. Needless to say the infection was knocked right out. I continued with my therapy. Making progress most days while I was in therapy, the Lord used me there to give some of the other patients hope, and to help them to want to work harder on their exercises there at the office and at home. My therapist asked me to come in and talk to a couple of her patients that were getting down and just didn't want to give it their all—because they saw no hope. God blessed me with new friends through this. He also blessed me by letting me speak to these people to tell them what the Lord had done for me and had shown me through all that had happened. Their faces and their progress showed hope and life and happiness.

Now I was doing therapy. I was doing my exercises at home. Satan is starting to show his ugly face again. It starts setting in that I am scared for life. I would sit and look at my arm and think, "How gross it looks." I would wonder what people are going to say when they see it. I would wonder if it was going to embarrass my family.

My friend and I went to a restaurant in another county. When we walked in and went to sit at our table, I slid all the way over to the wall and put my arm under the table. My friend asked me why I was doing that; she could tell I was going to extremes to hide it. I told her, "Nobody wants to sit in a place to eat and look at something this gross." She said, "It is not gross; it is a blessing. Stop hiding it." The waitress walked up and boldly asked, "What is she hiding." My friend started telling her about my accident. The waitress placed her hand over her mouth and said,

"I know who you are—you are the lady who blew her arm off in the tire shop in Pulaski." I said, "Excuse me?" She said, "You are the lady who was in the bad accident." I said, "Yes, I am." She started yelling across the restaurant for the other waitresses to come over there. When they got there, she told them who I was. They started telling me what a blessing I was. I told them, "I owe it all to God." The waitress said, "You do not need to hide that arm. That is a blessing. You don't hide blessings."

I continued with my therapy. I had gotten it down to two days a week.

I was making great progress. The doctor released me to go back to work on August the seventh.

I went to work. People would come to me and speak to me about the Lord's grace for me. It was overwhelming to see the people that would come by where I worked when they heard I was back—to have them come back there and hug me, worshiping the Lord and Savior. It was so awesome to witness. I would have people to come to me and hug me and thank me for showing them such blessings. I would tell them it wasn't me. The Lord is speaking to you through all this. I would have people to come up to me and would ask, what happened to that woman that died when that tire exploded. To see the look on their face when I would say, "I'm still here."

I had a lady come to the shop; she hugged me with all her might, crying uncontrollable, and told me, "Thank you." I said, "For what?" She said her husband, who is one of my best customers, had never spoken of God never prayed to God. As soon as he heard of my accident, her husband hit his knees and prayed and cried so hard. I told her, "God did that. Not me. I'm just a vessel."   Satan tried his best to get in there, too. I had a lady to see my arm and she just plainly asked what did you do try to commit suicide and just did a bad job of it. I took her by the arm and I said, "You got a minute? I would love to tell you a story." Minutes later Satan was defeated—again.

Therapy had gotten down to one day a week. The trail of tears is coming on strong. I'm getting nervous, but I have every intention of being in it. I look back at everything and the things I see are so remarkable, so amazing, how God is in all this. Yes it was a trauma, and yes it changed my life forever. I will never be the same. I'm not going to lie; Satan still sticks his head in from time to time. I look back further than the accident and see God prepared me for this a long time so that I could accept him into my heart; with that, he gave me life for eternity. Then he filled me with his knowledge so I could be prepared spiritually. He placed people in my life—like this one man I worked with who is disabled on one side. I would ask him over a period of time how he would do daily things differently with just one arm. Believe me; it all came in handy while I was able to only use my left arm. God helped me to touch so many people daily. I was truly blessed with friends and Christians praying for me and lifting me up in my time of need. Satan still managed to get through the crack in this event but, praise God, my faith has been strong; with that, I'm able to strike him down. God is good.

God sent me another confir-mation—I think he did it to keep

me strong. The angel, that I thought was a nurse in Vanderbilt while I was in the trauma unit, had told me the reason the people were crying on the other side of the curtain was because the patient was a logger and a tree he had cut jumped back and took off half his face. His family was telling him goodbye, because they had to unplug him.

Well, one day, a lady I worked with was having her horse looked at and having horseshoes put on. The man who was doing the work started talking to her and, as they talked, he began to talk about his brother. His brother had been in a logging accident—a tree had jumped back and had taken off half of his face. She looked at him and said, "Was that March 2010?" He said, "Yeah, how did you know?" He said, "We had to unplug his machine because he wasn't going to live." She said, "My friend was there, too. A tire had blown up on her, and had taken her right arm almost completely off." He said, "I remember her." Wow! Small world! God is good!

The Trail of Tears had come around and, yes, praise the Lord, I was in it. I enjoyed every second of it. I praise God that my special time with him was not robbed from me through this trauma. I have ridden every year since then, praising the Lord all the way.

The therapy has stopped. I am back to doing my normal stuff in life. I look at things totally differently now. I see things through a whole new way now. I never take it for granted I have tomorrow. I never take it for granted that I have all the time in the world to tell someone I love them. I try to enjoy and take in every precious moment with my son. I never take it for granted that I have all my body parts to function every day.

I often have wondered what I would have done if I hadn't had accepted Jesus in my heart in 1996. How would I have gotten through all this? Would I have had such an awesome blessing to rise from such a terrible trauma? I have often thought about all the times I should be giving time to Jesus and I'm just too busy. What would have happened that day if Jesus had just been too busy to be there for me?

According to Matthew 19:26, Jesus looked at them and said "With man this is impossible, but with God all things are possible."

I am so proud to be a follower of my Savior! He has done so much for me! He died on the cross for me and rose to give me eternity in Heaven! He carries me through my daily journey here on this earth! I never want to live a day without him!

ABOUT THE AUTHOR

Photo by Denise Dillon

Christie Layne is a wife, mother, and survivor of a horrendous explosion. More than that, she is a devoted follower of her Lord, Jesus Christ.

Christie rides her motorcycle annually in the Trail of Tears as her testimony to the wonderful grace of God.